Financial Aid
Smarts
Getting Money for School

Lisa McCormick

ROSEN
PUBLISHING®

New York

Published in 2013 by The Rosen Publishing Group, Inc.
29 East 21st Street, New York, NY 10010

Library of Congress Cataloging-in-Publication Data

McCormick, Lisa Wade.
Financial aid smarts: getting money for school/Lisa Wade McCormick.—1st ed.
    p. cm.—(Get smart with your money)
Includes bibliographical references and index.
ISBN 978-1-4488-8252-6 (library binding)—
ISBN 978-1-4488-8266-3 (pbk.)—
ISBN 978-1-4488-8267-0 (6-pack)
1. College costs—United States—Planning—Juvenile literature.
2. Student aid—United States—Juvenile literature. 3. Education, Higher—United States—Finance—Juvenile literature. I. Title.
LB2342.M373 2013
378.30973—dc23

2012024847

Manufactured in the United States of America

CPSIA Compliance Information: Batch #W13YA: For further information, contact Rosen Publishing, New York, New York, at 1-800-237-9932.

Contents

Introduction

Concerns about the soaring costs of college hit close to home for a senior at the University of Illinois in Chicago. The aspiring occupational therapist told CBS News that she constantly worries about the $50,000 debt she'll have when she graduates.

"It's really overwhelming," she said during an October 2011 interview. "As much as I don't want to think about it, I have to think about it."

High school and college students across the country echo those fears. Skyrocketing costs have made many of these future leaders wonder if they can afford college. Others worry they'll be saddled with thousands of dollars in student loan debt after they graduate.

A 2011 study shed light on the rising costs of a college degree. The annual "Trends in College Pricing" report revealed that tuition and fees at four-year public schools jumped 8.3 percent in 2011 to an average of $8,244. That was twice the rate of inflation. With room and board, the price tag climbed to $17,131.

Students at private four-year institutions had to dig deeper into their pocketbooks, too. The total costs of those schools rose to $38,589, according to the report by the College Board. The nonprofit association does

More than nineteen million students enrolled in U.S. colleges and universities in 2011, according to the Census Bureau. Finding money to pay for school is a major concern among those students.

research and advocacy work for students, teachers, and others in the educational community.

There appears to be no end in sight to these soaring prices. Experts predict that in 2012–13 tuition will jump at least 3 percent at private schools and 5 percent at public schools. Some public universities may charge a premium of up to 30 percent for high-demand classes, according to a 2012 report by *Money* magazine.

How can students and their families keep up with these rising costs? How can they find "free" money—like grants and scholarships—to pay for college instead of relying on expensive loans?

Do your homework, financial aid experts say. Find out how the financial process works. And learn ways to tap into all the possible sources of money.

"College can be more affordable than you might think," author Lynn O'Shaughnessy says in her book *The College Solution*.

Private colleges and universities, for example, reduce tuition for students they want in their programs. Those discounts average about 33.5 percent, the College Board said.

Many students also pay much less than the advertised sticker price for college. "The average tuition discount for public schools, which cost less to begin with, is nearly 15 percent," says O'Shaughnessy.

Students should also compare prices. Costs differ from state to state. Financial aid packages vary, too.

In 2010–11, undergraduate students received an average of $12,455 per student in financial aid, according to the College Board. The average financial aid package included $6,539 in grants, $4,907 in federal loans, and $1,009 in tax credits and deductions and federal work-study.

Students may still be buried in debt when they graduate, financial aid experts say. But the benefits of a college degree outweigh those expenses.

College graduates are more likely to find a job than those with just a high school diploma. The unemployment rate for recent college graduates hovered around 8.9 percent, according to a 2012 report by the Georgetown Center on Education and the Workforce.

The unemployment rate for high school graduates? A staggering 22.9 percent.

College graduates also make more than those with a high school diploma. "The difference in lifetime earning power between a student who stops with a high school education and someone who earns a bachelor's degree is roughly $1.2 million," says O'Shaughnessy.

In the next few chapters, we'll show you how and where to find money for college, including sources some students may overlook. We'll also tell you why financial aid experts say college is still within every student's financial reach.

"Whoever you are, there is financial aid available," says Haley Chitty, spokesman for the National Association of Student Financial Aid Administrators.

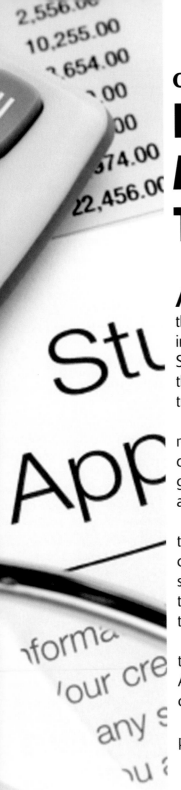

Chapter 1

How Do I Start My Financial Aid Treasure Hunt?

A group of high school students in Virginia received troubling news in April 2012 about the spiraling costs of a college degree. Standing inside a packed gymnasium at Maury High School, Vice President Joe Biden told the seniors that tuition at public four-year colleges had tripled during their lifetimes.

The vice president had more worrisome news on that Tuesday morning for these future doctors, engineers, and teachers. Many college graduates, he said, are burdened with an average of $25,000 in student loan debt.

The news struck a chord with students in that Norfolk, Virginia, gymnasium. It also hit close to home for millions of college-bound students and their families nationwide, especially those who are strapped for cash during these tough economic times.

"Recession-battered parents have less money to spend on their kids' tuition," according to an April 21, 2011, Associated Press article. "And college prices keep going up."

What, if anything, can students and their parents do to offset those rising prices? How can

Vice President Joe Biden talked to students at Maury High School in Virginia about the soaring costs of a college degree. He said the government should ensure that college is affordable for every American.

they pay the $80,000 or more it often costs to attend college for four years?

They need a financial aid game plan, experts say. They need to learn how the long and tedious financial aid process works and tip the money scales in their favor.

Learn the Financial Aid Language

But first, students and their parents need to learn the language spoken in the world of financial aid. It's a language riddled with complicated words and unfamiliar acronyms.

Here are some common phrases:

College Scholarship Service Profile (CSS/Financial Aid Profile): A financial aid profile used by some colleges to determine nonfederal financial aid.

cost of attendance (COA): An estimate of a student's total educational-related expenses during the college year. Those costs usually include tuition, fees, books, supplies, and basic living expenses. They vary from school to school.

expected family contribution (EFC): The government's estimate of how much money a family can afford to spend in one year for their child's college education.

College students like Tiphanie Yanique participate in work-study programs to help pay for school. Tiphanie and other students waited tables as part of their work-study at Middlebury College in Vermont.

Free Application for Federal Student Aid (FAFSA): A form used to determine a student's eligibility for federal financial aid and some state and private funds.

grant: A type of financial aid that does not have to be repaid.

interest: The cost of borrowing money.

loan: A type of financial aid that must be repaid with interest.

scholarship: Financial aid based on merit or ability. Scholarships do not have to be repaid. Funds usually come from colleges or private sources.

Student Aid Report (SAR): A report that indicates a student's expected family contribution. Colleges use this report to determine how much financial aid a student is eligible to receive.

tuition: The instructional fees charged by a college or university.

work-study: A student jobs program provided through colleges. Students usually work up to twenty hours a week.

How Does the System Work?

The next step in this journey to college funds is to learn the system. How does it work? How does the government decide who is eligible for financial aid—and how much?

There are two types of financial aid given to students. One is called merit assistance. This is based on students' abilities in such areas as music, science, sports, and academics. It can be tied to a student's major in college, too. Merit aid doesn't usually have to be repaid. Students, however, are often required to have a certain grade point average or meet other standards to receive and keep the money. Scholarships are a common type of merit aid.

The second type of financial assistance is need-based aid.

"The amount of need-based aid you receive depends on how much you and your family can afford to pay toward your college expense," according to *College Financing Information for Teens*. Students and their families are expected to help cover some college costs, financial aid experts say.

According to the Missouri Department of Higher Education, there is a federal formula used to determine a student's financial need. That formula is:

Cost of Attendance (COA) – Expected Family Contribution = Financial Need.

The cost figure in that equation is a critical piece in the financial aid puzzle, experts say. "How much assistance a family can snag will be dramatically different if the school is modestly priced or breathtakingly expensive," author Lynn O'Shaughnessy says in *The College Solution*.

Let's say, for example, that John wants to attend a school that costs $10,000 a year and his family's EFC is $15,000. In that scenario, John's family would be expected to pay the entire bill for college.

Why? The school costs less than his family's EFC.

But if John wants to attend a college that costs $50,000 a year and his family's EFC is $15,000, he could be eligible for up to $35,000 in financial aid.

Parents who have more than one child in college should receive even more financial assistance, according to O'Shaughnessy. In those cases, the parent's EFC is divided by the number of children attending college. The lower the EFC, the more financial aid students can receive.

FAFSA Made Simple

But how does the government calculate that magical EFC number? How does it decide the amount of money families can or should contribute to their children's college education?

Beware of Identity Thieves

Students need to protect their personal information from identity thieves, financial aid experts say. Identity theft is rampant across the country. College campuses are no exception. Students need safeguards to prevent criminals from assuming their identities and destroying their credit. Never share your Social Security number or other personal or financial information with anyone. Shred credit card statements and any documents that contain personal information. Ask if your school uses your Social Security number as a student identification number. If it does, ask for another number.

Everything is based on a form called the Free Application for Federal Student Aid, or FAFSA. The FAFSA is a student's ticket to federal financial aid, scholarships, work-study, and some private and state funds. It's the gateway to college money.

The FAFSA must be filled out annually—months before students begin their next academic year. The form should be submitted as close to January 1 as possible and preferably before February 15. Students can check federal and state FAFSA deadlines at the FAFSA Web site (http://www.fafsa.ed.gov).

Financial aid experts say the earlier students and parents submit their FAFSA the more money they'll likely receive. Many states award financial aid on a first-come, first-served basis.

"They have a limited pool of funds and when they run out of money, they stop awarding money," says Mark Kantrowitz, publisher of FinAid.org and FastWeb.com.

In her book, O'Shaughnessy warns parents of high school seniors not to wait until the last minute to fill out the FAFSA.

"You'll be taking a great risk if you wait to run the numbers until the real deadline for graduating seniors," she says.

Online Financial Aid Calculators

Many online calculators can give parents an early idea of how much—if any—financial aid their children may receive.

Don't Get Duped

The U.S. Department of Education warns students and their parents to be wary of companies that "guarantee" they can find scholarships or charge hefty fees for financial aid services that are available for free. Those companies often use high-pressure sales tactics or misrepresent their services. During your search for college funds, beware of companies that make the following claims:

- "Buy now or miss this opportunity": Never let anyone pressure you into making a quick decision. And don't pay for financial aid information that's free from other sources.
- "We guarantee you'll get aid": No one can make that guarantee. Some financial aid services charge consumers more than $1,000 and claim

they fulfilled their promises by finding a $250 scholarship. According to FinAid.com, scholarship scams dupe students and parents out of more than $100 million each year.

- "I've got aid for you; give me your financial information": Never give your credit card or bank account numbers to unknown companies that solicit you over the phone, through e-mail, or regular mail.

Several Web sites also offer to help students and their parents fill out the FAFSA. But those Web sites charge steep fees for their services.

The official FAFSA Web site answers questions and processes the form free of charge.

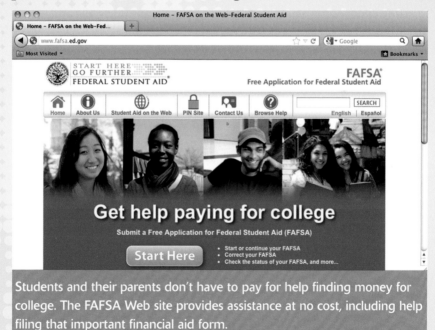

Students and their parents don't have to pay for help finding money for college. The FAFSA Web site provides assistance at no cost, including help filing that important financial aid form.

Parents should run preliminary numbers when their children are sophomores or juniors in high school, according to O'Shaughnessy. The beginning of twelfth grade is a great time to start, before students actually begin applying to schools.

Online calculators, however, do not give exact financial aid figures, so keep that in mind as you begin working out finances for college.

Information Needed on the FAFSA

When parents and students are ready to fill out their FAFSA, they will need the following personal and financial information:

- Dates of birth.
- Social Security numbers.
- Family size.
- The number of children in college.
- If the student is listed as a dependent on parents' taxes.
- The previous year's tax returns.
- W-2 forms.
- Recent pay stub.
- A summary of assets in both the parent's and student's names. Assets include bank accounts, business records, mortgage information, stocks, bonds, and other investments.
- Records for any untaxed income, like veteran's benefits or child support.

Parents and students can estimate their taxes on the FAFSA and correct the information later, financial aid experts say. When filling out the form, never leave any questions blank. Put zeroes in boxes that don't apply to you or your financial situation. If you leave a box blank, the computer could miscalculate your EFC.

Financial aid experts said all families—regardless of their incomes—should fill out the FAFSA.

Some schools, however, won't award merit scholarships unless a student or his or her family have filled out the FAFSA. Students can't receive government financial aid if the form isn't filed, either.

What's Next?

The U.S. Department of Education processes the FAFSA in two to six weeks. This is a free service. The results—or a Student Aid Report (SAR)—are sent to the e-mail or street address listed on the FAFSA. They're also sent to the schools listed on that federal form.

The SAR is the key piece in the financial aid picture because it contains that important EFC figure—the index colleges use to determine how much financial aid students can receive. The lower the EFC, the more financial aid students should receive.

What happens if you don't receive enough financial to attend college? Review your FAFSA. It's estimated that 90

College students and their families must fill out and submit the FAFSA form to learn how much financial aid they'll receive. Students can't receive some types of financial aid if they don't file the form.

percent of families make mistakes on the form. Contact the colleges, too. They can make mistakes. Let the schools' financial aid officers know about any extenuating circumstances that you can't include on the FAFSA, like high medical bills or a disabled family member.

Here's the good news—almost every student qualifies for some type of financial aid.

The money is out there. Students just need to know where to look and when to start their financial aid treasure hunts.

CHAPTER 2
It Pays to Plan Ahead

The question was simple and direct. It came from a high school sophomore hoping to get into one of the country's top universities.

"I was wondering when I should start looking into financial aid," the teenager asked on an online forum.

The sooner, the better, financial aid experts say. High school students need to know how the process of finding money for college works. They also need to know how to improve their odds of getting scholarships and grants— "free" college money that doesn't have to be repaid.

Freshman Year

These valuable lessons start when students are in the ninth grade. This is the year when high school students should get in the college mindset and explore how much it costs to get a four-year degree. Check out different college Web sites. Review the tuition and other fees—for in-state and out-of-state students. The prices may surprise many students.

During the 2011–12 school year, for example, in-state tuition for incoming freshman at the

High school students increase their odds of getting scholarships for college if they take challenging classes and keep their grades high. Many scholarships are based on students' grade point average.

University of Kansas (KU) was $8,364. With room and board, books, and other fees, the price jumped to approximately $17,500. The cost increased to $21,750 for out-of-state freshmen. It spiked to $30,894 with room and board and other expenses. Some Ivy League schools cost nearly twice that amount. The total cost of attendance at Princeton, for example, was a staggering $54,780 for the 2012–13 school year.

But don't let a college's advertised price scare you away. Most students receive scholarships, grants, loans, or work-study to help cover those high costs.

"You can't take the sticker prices at face value," says Haley Chitty, spokesman for the National Association of Student

Financial Aid Administrators. "The vast majority of students get some form of student aid that brings down the price."

During their ninth grade year, students should have the "money talk" with their parents. They need to know how much their parents can pay for college. Those discussions should help students narrow their college options.

Financial aid experts advise high school freshmen to enroll in challenging math, science, history, and English classes. Take a foreign language, too. And keep your grades up. Colleges look closely at students' grade point average when making admission decisions. Many scholarships and grants are tied to students' grades, too.

Ninth grade is an excellent time to research possible scholarships and contests that award cash prizes for college. Students can get information from high school counselors, local libraries, scholarship Web sites, and community organizations.

Freshmen should also try to get involved in extracurricular activities and do volunteer work in their communities. Those activities could give students possible leads on scholarships.

Finally, get organized. Create files for information about colleges and their costs, scholarship possibilities, and other college-related issues.

Sophomore Year

In their sophomore year in high school, students should take the preliminary SAT or ACT exams.

These college admissions tests measure students' knowledge in such subjects as reading, math, writing, and critical thinking. But the results don't count—not yet, anyway. Only the SAT and ACT tests that students take when they're juniors are used to determine possible scholarships.

Essay Writing Tips

Most colleges require students to include a personal essay with their applications. Many scholarships require them, too. Students who have a gift with words and can write engaging essays increase their odds of getting accepted into college and receiving much-needed scholarships.

But what about students who struggle with writing? How can they ensure their essays won't make an admissions counselor or scholarship adviser automatically write them off?

Here are some tips:

- Answer the question posed.
- Include personal information.
- Write an engaging lede that hooks the reader's interest.
- Use active verbs.
- Check your grammar and spelling. Don't rely solely on spell-check: it can't tell the difference between "there" and "their."
- Ask your English teacher to proofread your essay.
- Don't wait until the last minute. You don't want to rush.
- Avoid clichés.
- Use your own words; don't plagiarize someone else's.
- Stick to the word count.
- Don't use bullet points to list your achievements. Describe them in complete sentences.
- Write and rewrite.
- Don't use stilted prose. Write like you talk.

Students can take the Preliminary Scholastic Aptitude Test (PSAT) in October of their sophomore year. Author Valerie Pierce, who wrote *Countdown to College: 21 'To Do' Lists for High School*, calls that test the "SAT's baby brother."

The PSAT is combined with the National Merit Scholarship Qualifying Test (NMSQT) and measures students' abilities in critical reading, math problem-solving skills, and writing.

Another test that sophomores can take to identify their academic strengths and weaknesses is called the PLAN—the Pre-American College Test. Pierce calls this test the "ACT's baby brother." The PLAN is given in October of a student's sophomore year. Not every school offers this test, though. Ask your school counselor for help finding a school that does.

College and financial aid experts say both tests are important because they:

- Give students firsthand experience at taking the ACT or SAT
- Let students compare their results to other students applying for college
- Open the floodgates of information from colleges nationwide

During their sophomore year, students should think about where they'd like to go to college and what they'd like to study. There are more than 4,000 four-year public and private colleges in the United States and another 1,900 community colleges. Students need to consider what type of college they'd like to attend. Do they want one with stellar academic programs? What about small classes? Or are they targeting schools that offer the most financial aid?

Sophomores should make a list of the colleges they'd like to attend—and tour those schools. Be sure to meet with the financial aid officers. Find out how much assistance most students receive and if those aid packages are guaranteed for more than one year. Students should also ask if certain restrictions apply, like maintaining a specific grade point average.

Finally, sophomores need to keep their grades up. In her book, Pierce ranked—in order of importance—what colleges look for in their students:

1). Grade point average and class rank

2). SAT/ACT scores

3). Extracurricular activities, college essays, and teachers'/ counselors' recommendations

Junior Year

With only two years left in high school, a student's junior year is "crunch time." This is the year when high school students take their ACTs or SATs, attend college fairs, go on more college tours, write essays for college applications, intensify their search for scholarships, and make sure their grades don't slide.

"College admission folks rely heavily on your junior year GPA," Pierce says in her book. "They want to see rising—not falling."

Juniors should consider taking Advanced Placement (AP) classes. Find out if you can receive college credit for those courses. It's possible for high school students to graduate with ten to fifteen hours of college credit. That adds up to significant savings because it cuts the length of time students need to earn their college degrees.

Juniors should narrow their college picks to five to twenty schools, experts say. Request information packets from those colleges and zero in on the cost-of-attendance figures. Juniors need to spend more time looking for scholarships, too. Focus on ones that match your talents and passions. High school juniors should also study and register for the ACTs and SATs. Most colleges accept both tests.

The American College Testing—or ACT—measures students' knowledge in English, math, reading, and science. It has an

College-bound students should take the ACT or SAT during high school. Students who ace these academic achievement tests often receive top-dollar scholarships. Students can take the tests multiple times to increase their scores.

optional writing test, too. The approximately 3.5-hour test includes 215 multiple-choice questions. It's given six times during the school year. A perfect score on the ACT is 36.

The SAT measures students' reasoning abilities in reading and math. It also tests students' writing skills. The test is three hours and forty-five minutes and is given seven times a year. A perfect SAT score is 2400.

Students who don't do well on the tests can take them again. "Studies show that you can increase your score as much as 20 percent, but not without studying," Pierce wrote in her book.

Students who ace the ACT or SAT increase their odds of getting into college and receiving top-dollar scholarships.

During their junior year in high school, students also need to learn how the financial aid system works.

"The more you understand financial aid, the more likely you are to receive it," Pierce says in her book.

Senior Year

When students enter their senior year in high school, they face what Pierce calls "deadlines, details, and decisions." Those three D's apply to which college students will attend and how they'll pay the bill.

Make a master calendar to keep track of everything. Highlight such dates as retakes for the SATs or ACTs and deadlines for college and scholarship applications and submitting financial aid information.

The FAFSA deadline is the most important date for high school seniors—and their parents. This federal form can be filed on January 1 of the student's senior year in high school. Students have a better chance to receive financial aid if their parents submit the FAFSA early.

Schools like Bronx Community College in New York are excellent options for students who can't afford a more expensive four-year university. Community colleges usually have less stringent admission requirements than traditional four-year schools, too.

High school males, however, can't receive any financial aid if they don't register for the Selective Service draft when they turn eighteen. Women aren't required to register.

One question that high school seniors should consider is whether they're going to take the "early decision" option offered by some colleges. This option lets students apply early—and find out early if they're accepted.

27

Financial aid experts caution students about taking that route to college.

"Research shows that applicants who commit to one college early tend to get less aid money than those who wait and end up with acceptance offers from several schools," according to an article in the April 2012 issue of *Money*. "That's especially true for students vying for merit scholarships."

High school seniors should know by March or April which colleges have accepted their applications. Be sure to compare financial aid packages before making a final decision.

May 1 is national decision day for most high school seniors. It's the day—or close to the day—when students must decide which college they're going to attend.

What about seniors who still can't afford a traditional four-year school? Or students who didn't get accepted because of their grades? What options do they have?

One alternative is community college. Other options are technology or trade schools.

"There are multiple paths students can take to college," says Chitty. "They shouldn't get discouraged if they don't get a full ride to Harvard."

Myths & Facts

Myth   Only athletes get full-ride scholarships to college.

Fact   This varies by institution, but there are many high-dollar scholarships available to students who excel academically.

Myth   I can't afford to go to college because my family is poor.

Fact   Financial aid is available to everyone, regardless of their financial background. Students have to be smart to find assistance, but it is available.

Myth   I'm not eligible for financial aid because my parents make too much money.

Fact   Just about everyone can get some type of federal student aid. All students should fill out the Free Application for Federal Student Aid because they never know what assistance they could be eligible to receive. Students also can't receive any federal financial aid or many scholarships if the FAFSA isn't filled out. Families that have more than one student in college will see a decrease in the amount of money they're expected to contribute. That means their financial aid could increase.

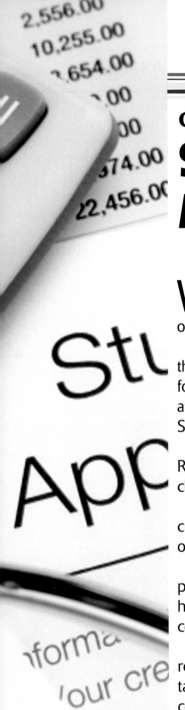

Chapter 3

Show Me the Money

Who would imagine that a jar of peanut butter could help students pay the escalating costs of college?

As crazy as it sounds, it's possible. Just ask the South Carolina student who won $35,000 for her P-Nutty BBQ Chicken Quesadilla creation in Jif's Most Creative Peanut Butter Sandwich Contest.

"Good news, I'm going to college!" Mallory Russell told her classmates after her sandwich claimed top prize in the 2012 nationwide contest.

Mallory's "slice of life" story illustrates the creative ways that some students are cashing in on much-needed money for college.

But what about students who aren't champion sandwich makers? Or students who don't have perfect grades? Can they find money for college?

Financial aid experts say most students—regardless of their grades or talents—are able to tap into some public and private funds for college.

"The majority of full-time students receive aid—nearly two-thirds got grants or scholarships

Sasha Khmeinik checked out the vehicle she designed for the Peak Performance competition sponsored by Boston University's College of Engineering. Top prize was a $20,000 scholarship. Many students enter competitions to win money for college.

in 2007–08, the most recent data available," reported *Money*. "Average amount: just over $7,000."

But there's the problem: $7,000 won't cover one year's tuition at most colleges in the United States. Students and their parents must scramble to find other sources of financial aid to cover the skyrocketing costs of college.

What options do they have?

Let's start our financial aid treasure hunt with the federal government, which awards money through work-study programs, loans, and grants.

Federal Grants

The federal government awards billions of dollars each year in grants to college students. These funds are highly coveted because they don't have to be repaid.

The most common federal grant is the Pell Grant. This grant is the "foundation of federal student financial aid," according to the Missouri Department of Higher Education.

Pell Grants are based solely on need. They're designed to give students from lower-income families access to college.

Military Benefits

The U.S. military has several programs to help its members pay for college. A key military benefit is tuition assistance. This usually covers 100 percent of tuition and some fees for service members. The military offers loans and scholarships, too. These educational benefits are available to veterans, reserves, and members who are on active duty in all branches of the military. Check with your military adviser or college financial aid officer for more information.

The U.S. Department of Education awarded more than $35 billion in Pell Grants in 2011. The average grant was $3,800.

The maximum Pell Grant award for the 2012 school year was $5,500. To receive that amount, students had to be enrolled in college full-time or had a parent or guardian who died in the line of duty in Iraq or Afghanistan after September 11, 2001.

The Federal Supplemental Educational Opportunity Grant (FSEOG) is available to students with "exceptional financial need." Students can receive $100 to $4,000 under this grant. However, not all colleges and universities participate in the FSEOG program. Check with a college financial aid officer about availability.

The Iraq and Afghanistan Service Grant is offered to students who don't qualify for Pell Grants, but whose parent or guardian—serving in the military—died in either of those countries after September 11, 2001. The maximum award under this grant is $5,500.

The Teacher Education Assistance for College and Higher Education Grant (TEACH Grant) offers money to students who plan to teach full-time—in elementary or secondary schools—for at least four years after graduation. Students can receive up to $4,000 a year under this grant.

Federal Work-Study

The Federal Work-Study (FWS) program finds part-time jobs for students to help them pay for college.

"The program encourages community service work and work related to the recipient's course of study," according to the U.S. Department of Education. Students are paid minimum wage and usually work ten to fifteen hours a week. Most students work on campus. Some work off-campus for non-profit organizations and public agencies.

College student David Nalette works as a busboy during the summer to help pay for school. Financial aid rarely covers all college expenses. Most students and their families have to pay some costs out-of-pocket.

Federal Loans

Students and their parents can borrow money from the government to pay for college, too. These loans must be repaid with interest.

Federal Perkins Loans are given to needy students to help cover the costs of college. These loans have a 5 percent interest rate and are made through a college or university. When the loans are due, students repay the schools.

College students can borrow up to $5,500 annually—with a maximum of $27,500 while they're undergraduates—through this loan program. Students must start repaying these loans nine months after graduation.

Another type of federal loan is the Parent Loan for Undergraduate Students (PLUS). These loans are made directly to parents of dependent students. Parents can borrow the difference between the college's cost of attendance and the student's financial aid package. For example, if the school's cost of attendance is $10,000 and the student receives $6,000 in financial aid, parents can borrow up to $4,000. PLUS loans have an interest rate of 7.9 percent. The first payments are due sixty days after the final disbursement—or payout—of the funds.

A college-bound student and his dad fill out a school's financial aid form. Students should go after scholarship and grant monies first. Those don't have to be repaid. Loans must be repaid with interest.

Stafford Loans

The federal government also offers Stafford Loans to help students pay the rising costs of college. There are two types of Stafford Loans: subsidized and unsubsidized.

Subsidized Stafford Loans are given to students based on need. These loans had an interest rate of 3.4 percent in 2011. The government pays the interest on these loans while students are in school.

Off-the-Wall Scholarships

High school students don't have to be the next Albert Einstein to find money for college. There's plenty of college cash available to students who speak Klingon, are extremely tall, or have other unusual traits and talents.

Here are a few wacky scholarships available to students:

- Have a knack with duct tape? The Stuck at Prom Scholarship Contest awards $5,000 each to the couple who makes the most creative outfit for prom with duct tape.
- Stand head and shoulders above the crowd? Tall Clubs International offers a $1,000 scholarship to male students who are at least 6 feet 2 inches (1.9 meters) and female students who are at least 5 feet 10 inches (1.8 meters) Students have to write an essay entitled "What Being Tall Means to Me" to win.
- Drink milk? The Scholar Athlete Milk Moustache of the Year (SAMMY) awards $7,500 to a scholar athlete with leadership skills. Students also have to write a "Milk Experience" essay.
- Is your name last name Zolp? If it is, you can get a full-ride to Loyola University in Chicago.
- *Star Trek* fan? The Klingon Language Institute offers $500 to undergraduate students interested in studying any language—not just Klingon.

- **Can you quack like a duck? The Chick and Sophie Major Memorial Duck Calling Contest awards up to $2,000 to the high school senior who wins this "ducky" competition.**

Unsubsidized Stafford Loans are not based on students' needs. These loans had an interest rate of 6.8 percent in 2011. The first payments are due six months after a student graduates.

Students can borrow up to $5,500 in Stafford Loans during their freshman year, $6,500 when they're sophomores, and $7,500 when they are juniors and seniors.

Stafford Loans are an affordable way to help pay for college. Check out StaffordLoan.com for more information on financing college with the help of low-interest loans.

Always read the fine print before signing any loan agreement. Be sure you understand the terms of the loan, how much you're borrowing, and when your first payment is due.

Federal Scholarships

The federal government offers some scholarships, too. Most are given through governmental agencies such as the National Institutes of Health or the Department of Transportation. The amounts and terms of federal scholarships vary. Check with the federal agencies or a college financial aid officer for more information.

State Scholarships

Most states have scholarship programs to help students pay for college. Scholarships are given according to students' needs, special circumstances, and academic achievements.

In Missouri, for example, students who ace the ACT or SAT are eligible for the Bright Flight scholarship. This merit scholarship awards up to $3,000 annually to students who scored in the top 3 percent on those academic achievement tests.

Other Scholarship Options

Students can find an almost endless supply of scholarships through private sources, too. Schools, religious groups, non-profit organizations, and corporations offer a variety of scholarships to students.

But author Lynn O' Shaughnessy says there are some drawbacks to scholarships.

"Private scholarships are often only awarded for one year," she says. "So if you work really hard to win scholarships to cover your freshman year, you will still have to deal with three years of college costs."

Scholarships have another downside, too. They can jeopardize part of a student's financial aid. "Federal rules require that a school consider outside scholarship money when calculating its financial aid package," says O'Shaughnessy.

When looking for scholarships, O'Shaughnessy recommends that students target those offered by colleges and universities. "The school scholarships are often far more lucrative than what you can expect with a private scholarship and they typically last four years," she says.

Earning a college degree is the dream of students nationwide. But the dream carries a hefty price tag. Many students are saddled with debt when they graduate. Scholarships and grants can reduce those high costs.

Other financial aid experts recommend a different approach. They suggest students first look for scholarships offered by organizations and businesses in their communities. Many students overlook these local sources and focus their attention on national scholarships. But the odds of getting a scholarship from the local Elks Club are much higher than getting money from a national organization, financial experts says. Some local groups may only award $250 scholarships, but those dollars can add up to big savings for college.

When students are ready to cast a wider net, financial aid experts suggest they focus on scholarships that match their interests. Students in the performing arts, for example, might consider the Michael Jackson and Rhythm Nations Scholarships, which award up to $5,000.

Interested in computer technology? Check out the Apple Scholars program, which rewards high school seniors' computer savvy, creativity, and academic excellence with $2,000, an Apple Nano iPod, and a laptop for college.

Are you a student athlete? Colleges and universities offer scores of athletic scholarships. Student athletes should talk to their high school coaches about possible scholarships and check with the National Collegiate Athletic Association (NCAA). The NCAA awards about $2 billion annually in financial aid to students attending Division I and II schools.

But the competition for athletic scholarships is fierce. "Only a small minority of students get full ride scholarships for athletics," says Haley Chitty, spokesman for the National Association of Student Financial Aid Administrators.

Students should focus their efforts on academic achievement. National Merit Scholarships are an excellent option for academic all-stars. Those scholarships can slash college costs. National Merit Finalists at the University of Kansas, for example, can receive up to $10,000 a year in scholarships.

Private Grants and Contests

Millions of students receive grant money from state and private sources. In Missouri, for example, students who have lost a parent in military action since September 11, 2001, are eligible for thousands of dollars through the state's Wartime Veteran's Survivors Grant.

Students who are mathematically gifted can apply for grants through the American Math Society. If they're computer geniuses, they can combine those talents to find grants through the National Science Foundation. High school counselors, college financial aid officers, and online tools can help students find more information about grants and scholarships.

Many contests offer cash prizes for college, too. Prizes are awarded for everything from essay writing to mathematical problem-solving skills. Remember Mallory Russell, the student who won $35,000 for her peanut butter recipe? She has plenty of time to save for college. Mallory was eight when she won that "nutty" contest.

Chapter 4

Protect Your Financial Future

A college student in Maine can't escape the constant worries she has about paying for school. Those concerns haunt Sydney Keyser's every move—and every decision.

The nursing major at the University of New England turns down her friends' requests to go to the movies. She doesn't join them when they ask her out for lunch, either. Financial difficulties at home—her mom's unemployment and possible foreclosure of the family's house—forced Keyser to keep tabs on how much she borrows and spends at school. She puts a price tag on everything, including her tests.

"It's about dollars and cents," says Keyser. "You're thinking about what sort of career can get me what kind of income and how fast I can get started."

College students across the country share many of Keyser's financial concerns. Most of them know they'll be saddled with thousands of dollars in student loan debt when they graduate. According to the Project on Student Debt, the class of 2010 graduated with an average debt of $25,250 per student. As college costs continue to skyrocket, many students wonder what steps

Graduating from college is a milestone for students and their proud parents. College students who watch their spending and keep their grades up are less likely to be burdened with debt when they graduate.

they can take to protect their financial futures. What, if anything, can they do to slash their student loan debt and other college expenses?

Grades Still Matter

For starters, college students shouldn't let their grades slide. That's difficult for many students because college classes are often more challenging than high school courses. Many college freshmen are getting their first taste of freedom, too. Their grades may fall—at least temporarily—while they adjust to college life. But students need to remember that financial aid packages are directly tied to their grades. There's no guarantee that students will receive the same amount of financial aid as they did the previous year, especially if their grades plummet.

The federal government requires colleges and universities to review the academic progress of students who receive financial aid. Those students must demonstrate what is called satisfactory academic progress (SAP) to continue receiving federal, state, and some institutional sources of financial aid.

What Is Satisfactory Academic Progress?

At the University of Kansas, students must maintain a minimum grade point average of 2.0 and complete at least 75 percent of their cumulative attempted hours to demonstrate SAP.

These SAP standards are similar at colleges and universities across the country.

Students who don't meet their school's SAP—even after the first semester of their freshman year—face costly consequences. They're usually placed on "financial aid warning status" and could lose their grants, loans, and work-study if they don't meet their school's SAP by the end of their next term.

Many private scholarships and grants require students to meet certain academic standards, too. Let's say, for example, that a student must maintain a 3.5 GPA to keep a specific scholarship. If the student's GPA dips to even a 3.4, he or she risks losing the scholarship and its funding.

Students should check the requirements for every scholarship and grant they receive, financial aid experts say.

Keep Searching for Money

College students should never stop looking for scholarships or grants. Rules change. Doors open. New opportunities develop. Students shouldn't ignore internship opportunities, especially

College students can impress potential employers during their interviews if they have good résumés and communication skills. Students who work as interns during college can learn those skills. Internships also look great on résumés.

when they're juniors or seniors in college. Many internship programs pay students. Others offer college credit. Internships give students the chance to work in their fields of study. And they're often gateways to future jobs.

Loan Forgiveness Programs

Want the federal government to erase all or part of your student loans? How about a chance to earn thousands of dollars to help pay those costly college loans? These financial opportunities are available to students who work in certain professions or volunteer for specific organizations.

Students who volunteer for one year with AmeriCorps, for example, receive $4,725 to apply toward their college loans. They receive up to $7,400 in living expenses, too. AmeriCorps volunteers help local and national nonprofit groups fight illiteracy, clean parks, build affordable homes, and work on other community projects.

Peace Corps volunteers can get part of their federal Perkins Loans cancelled and—after two years of service—receive a $6,000 readjustment allowance. Students can use part of that allowance to pay their college loans.

Under the National Defense Education Act, students who become full-time teachers in schools that serve low-income communities can get up to 30 percent of their Perkins Loans forgiven.

The federal government has additional loan forgiveness programs for teachers and other professionals. These programs are available to college graduates who work full-time as special education teachers or to qualified professionals who teach math, science, foreign languages, bilingual education, or other subjects that have shortages of teachers.

Students who volunteer for such organizations as the Peace Corps can get some of their college loans forgiven. Natalie Galiotto, in the red shirt, taught English in Cambodia as a Peace Corps volunteer.

Many students, however, aren't aware of these programs. They often take out costly loans they could have avoided with a little planning and research. Ask your college financial aid officer for more information about these and other loan forgiveness programs.

Money Management 101

Another way that students can reduce their college debt is to set a budget—and stick to it—when they first arrive on campus. Otherwise, everyday spending can spiral out of control.

College Dreams Dashed for Most Undocumented Students

Thousands of undocumented students in the United States dream of going to college. But those dreams often turn into nightmares for these aspiring teachers, doctors, and lawyers.

Poor grades aren't the issue for these students.

It's their immigration status. They're in this country without legal documentation. They don't have a key piece of information that most colleges request on their application—a nine-digit Social Security number.

Undocumented students face other roadblocks on their higher-education journeys. By 2011, South Carolina and Alabama had banned undocumented immigrants from enrolling in public colleges and universities. And many four-year public colleges in Virginia refused to admit students who couldn't show proof of citizenship or legal residency.

Undocumented students face an even bigger obstacle in their pursuit of a college degree: money. Many undocumented students live below the poverty line. Their families don't have the financial resources to pay for college. And financial aid isn't an option. Undocumented students can't legally receive federal or state financial aid, including grants, work-study, or loans. They aren't eligible for many scholarships, either.

But each year, seven thousand to thirteen thousand undocumented students beat those college odds. They find schools that will accept them—in spite of their status.

They also tap into the few scholarships that don't require a Social Security number or legal status.

Undocumented students who want to pursue a college degree should talk to their high school counselors. They can also contact immigration advocacy groups like Educators for Fair Consideration for college advice and assistance.

According to officials at the University of Minnesota, the first year of college is the first time students must learn to control their own finances. College freshmen, for example, may not understand how quickly those $3 mocha lattes or late-night runs for pizza can drain their savings. But those expenses soon add up to staggering amounts.

Just how much?

A 2010 study by Alloy Media + Marketing projected that annual discretionary—or optional—spending among eighteen- to twenty-four-year-old college students nationwide would total $37.7 billion. That's an average of $361 per student—per month—or $4,332 annually in nonacademic purchases.

Expenses for students who live off-campus are even higher, financial aid experts warn. Those students must factor costs such as rent, utilities, and groceries into their budgets. For example, students who lived off-campus in San Francisco, California, were projected to spend a minimum of $14,030 in living expenses for nine months, according to 2012 figures released by the College Board.

Cutting College Costs

How can students cut those high costs? How can they slice spending without jeopardizing their college experience?

"Students need to live as cheaply as they can when they're in school," says Haley Chitty, spokesman for the National Association of Student Financial Aid Administrators.

Money magazine recommended several cost-cutting measures, including:

- No concierge service: Colleges offer many extras to make students' lives easier. But those laundry and pickup services are expensive. Students can do those jobs themselves and save hundreds of dollars.
- Buy used furniture: Students don't need new beds and dressers for their dorm rooms.
- Leave your car at home: It's expensive to park on a college campus. The 2012 annual parking fee at Harvard University was $1,356.
- Watch your gadget budget: In 2011, freshmen spent an average of $960 on laptop computers. More affordable refurbished computers are available at TigerDirect.com or Apple.com.
- Shop at big-box stores: Stock up on Gatorade, soap, toothpaste, snacks, and school supplies at stores like Target or Costco.
- Set spending limits: Make a pact to only spend $100 for sweatshirts and other clothes with the school's logos.
- Look for off-campus meal deals: The average student spent $765 in 2012 to eat at restaurants off-campus. Students can cut those costs with coupons and strict spending limits.
- Ask for student discounts: Movie theaters, restaurants, bookstores, and other retailers offer discounts to college students.
- Buy used books: Students can save 50 percent on books by buying used ones instead of new. Some

Web sites rent books. Others offer textbook downloads.

- Get a roommate if you live off-campus: You can save even more if you have more than one roommate.
- Don't buy the most expensive meal plan: Why pay for a meal plan that includes breakfast if you skip that meal? Find a plan that fits your eating habits.
- Go Greek: It's sometimes cheaper to join sororities or fraternities, especially if they have meal plans.
- Become a resident adviser (RA): Many schools offer free room and board to RAs. This is a good job for students who have leadership skills and can resolve conflicts.

One way to save money when you are entering college is to live with a roommate. In addition to saving money, you may end up with a friend for life when college is over.

Credit Card Warning

The widespread use of credit cards poses another financial nightmare for college students.

A 2012 study revealed the use of credit cards has "snowballed in the last decade" among college students. The study in the *International Journal of Business and Social Science* discovered the average college student in 2004 had $946 in credit card debt. That figure more than quadrupled to $4,100 by 2009.

"In America, credit cards on campus have been a disaster, leaving students buried in debt before graduation, often with little hope of paying off the debt before high fees and interest double the amount," the study said.

College students should only use credit cards in cases of emergency, financial aid experts say. Students should also pay off their credit cards each month to avoid high interest rates and other costly fees.

A Final Lesson on College Saving

Students who really want to cut their college costs should take a lesson from Sydney Keyser. She's the nursing student in Maine who learned to live on a tight budget. What's her secret?

She watches every penny she spends. She looks for free entertainment opportunities, like playing video games. And she hangs out with friends who are just as worried as she is about spending money.

Ten Great Questions to Ask
a FINANCIAL AID EXPERT

1 What sources of financial aid are available?

2 What are the deadlines for those different types of aid?

3 What requirements do I have to meet to become eligible for scholarships and grants? What about loans?

4 What scholarships are available in my community?

5 Where can I find information about national scholarships?

6 Where can I find information about writing an essay for college and scholarship applications?

7 When is the ACT or SAT given in my area?

8 Where can I get help to prepare for the ACT or SAT?

9 What are the repayment terms on my student loan?

10 Can I rent my college textbooks? What about used textbooks?

Glossary

acronym A word that is formed from the initials of several words.

concierge Someone who assists other people; a person in a hotel who helps guests.

cumulative Describing something that gradually builds up.

discretionary Optional; describing something that is based on a person's judgment.

extenuating Making something appear less serious; to justifying.

extracurricular Relating to activities at school that are not part of regular classes; outside activities.

foreclosure Legal action to take someone's home away. This is usually because the owner did not make the payments.

formula A plan or method for doing something.

index An indicator or sign of something; a number that expresses a relationship.

inflation Higher prices.

intensify To increase effort or concentrate on something.

jeopardize To put someone or something at risk.

plagiarize To copy someone else's work and claim it as your own.

plummet To suddenly and quickly drop.

preliminary Pertaining to something that is said or done early.

proficiencies Things that are done with a high degree of skill.

recession A decline in economic activity.

strategic Pertaining to a planned move or a careful decision.

vie To compete with someone or for something.

wary Cautious or suspicious.

For More Information

AmeriCorps
1201 New York Avenue NW
Washington, DC 20525
(202) 606-5000
Web site: http://www.americorps.gov
AmeriCorps provides nearly seventy-five thousand volunteers
each year to nonprofit and community groups working in
such areas as education, the environment, public safety,
and homeland security. Students who volunteer for one
year in AmeriCorps receive $4,725, which can be used
to pay for college or repay student loans.

College Board
45 Columbus Avenue
New York, NY 10023-6917
(212) 713-8000
Web site: http://www.collegeboard.org
This nonprofit membership association represents more than
5,900 colleges and universities. Its Web site has information for students about picking a college, planning for
college, and financial aid. It is designed to help college-
bound students weave their way through the daunting
challenge of getting ready for college and finding money
to pay for school.

Educators for Fair Consideration
2130 Fillmore Street, #248
San Francisco, CA 94115
Web site: http://www.e4fc.org
The mission of this California-based nonprofit organization is to
help undocumented students go to college and achieve

their professional dreams. The organization provides scholarships of up to $10,000 to help low-income undocumented students in the San Francisco area. It also has a wealth of information about scholarships specifically for undocumented students.

FinAid.org
P.O. Box 2056
Cranberry Township, PA 16066-1056
(724) 538-4500
Web site: http://www.finaid.org
This Web site bills itself as the "smartest student guide" to financial aid. It has information for students and parents about loans, scholarships, grants, the FAFSA, cost calculators, and military aid. It also has an "Ask the Aid Adviser" section for personalized help.

Military.com
622 Third Avenue, 39th Floor
New York, NY 10017
(212) 351-7000
Web site: http://www.military.com
Military.com, a business unit of Monster Worldwide, Inc., is the largest military and veteran online news and membership organization. It has information about the educational benefits offered to members of the military. Those educational benefits—offered to service members in all branches of the armed forces—include scholarships, tuition assistance, and a loan forgiveness program.

National Association of Student Financial Aid Administrators
1101 Connecticut Avenue NW, Suite 1100
Washington, DC 20036-4303

(202) 785-0453

Web site: http://www.nasfaa.org/students/About_Financial_
Aid.aspx

This is an organization for financial aid professionals. Its goal is
to help students achieve their educational dreams by
finding ways to pay for college. The organization stays
up-to-date on college-related issues and advocates for
students' financial interests at the college, state, and
federal levels. The Web site has an entire section filled
with information about financial aid for college students.

United Negro College Fund
8260 Willow Oaks Corporate Drive
P.O. Box 10444
Fairfax, VA 22031-8044
(800) 331-2244

Web site: http://www.uncf.org

This charitable educational organization helps more than sixty
thousand students each year go to college. It awards
hundreds of scholarships, internships, and fellowships to
students from low- and moderate-income backgrounds.
The organization has a list of possible scholarships on its
Web site.

Web Sites

Due to the changing nature of Internet links, Rosen Publishing
has developed an online list of Web sites related to the subject
of this book. This site is updated regularly. Please use this link
to access the list:

http://www.rosenlinks.com/GSM/Fina

For Further Reading

Bellenir, Karen. *College Financing Information for Teens: Tips for a Successful Financial Life*. Detroit, MI: Omnigraphics, 2008.

Bissonnette, Zac. *Debt-Free U: How I Paid for an Outstanding College Education Without Loans, Scholarships, or Mooching Off My Parents*. New York, NY: Portfolio Trade, 2010.

Brown, Nathan, and Sheryle A. Proper. *The Everything Paying for College Book*. Avon, MA: Adams Media, 2005.

Chaney, Kalman. *Paying for College Without Going Broke*. Framingham, MA: Princeton Review, 2011.

The College Board. *Getting Financial Aid 2012*. New York, NY: The College Board, 2011.

The College Board. *Scholarship Handbook 2012*. New York, NY: The College Board, 2011.

Kaplan, Benjamin. *How to Go to College Almost for Free*. New York, NY: Collins Reference, 2001.

Newport, Cal. *How to Be a High School Superstar: A Revolutionary Plan to Get into College by Standing Out (Without Burning Out)*. New York, NY: Three Rivers Press, 2010.

Orr, Tamara B. *America's Best Colleges for B Students: A College Guide for Students Without Straight A's*. Belmont, CA: Supercollege, 2011.

O'Shaughnessy, Lynn. *The College Solution: A Guide for Everyone Looking for the Right School at the Right Price*. Upper Saddle River, NJ: FT Press, 2008.

Pierce, Valerie, and Cheryl Rilly. *Countdown to College: 21 'To Do' Lists for High School*. Lansing, MA: Front Porch Press, 2009.

Princeton Review. *The Best Value Colleges, 2012 Edition: The 150 Best-Buy Schools and What It Takes to Get In*. Framingham, MA: Princeton Review, 2012.

Princeton Review. *College Essays That Made a Difference.* Framingham, MA: Princeton Review, 2010.

Princeton Review. *The Complete Book of College.* Framingham, MA: Princeton Review, 2011.

Princeton Review. *Cracking the ACT.* Framingham, MA: Princeton Review, 2011.

Princeton Review. *1,296 ACT Practice Questions.* Framingham, MA: Princeton Review, 2011.

Tanabe, Gen, and Kelly Tanabe. *How to Write a Winning Scholarship Essay: 30 Essays That Won Over $3 Million in Scholarships.* Belmont, CA: Supercollege, 2009.

Tanabe, Gen, and Kelly Tanabe. *1001 Ways to Pay for College.* Belmont, CA: Supercollege, 2011.

Tanabe, Gen, and Kelly Tanabe. *The Ultimate Scholarship Book 2012: Billions of Dollars in Scholarships, Grants and Prizes.* Belmont, CA: Supercollege, 2011.

Yale Daily News Staff. *The Insider's Guide to the Colleges, 2012: Students on Campus Tell You What You Really Want to Know.* New York, NY: St. Martin's Griffin, 2011.

Bibliography

Arnold, Chris. "Hard Financial Lessons Learned in College." NPR.org, May 19, 2011. Retrieved May 2012 (http://www.npr.org/2011/05/19/136243733/hard-financial-lessons-learned-in-college).

Ballenger, Brandon. "25 Bizarre Scholarships." *Money Talks News*, April 18, 2011. Retrieved May 2012 (http://www.moneytalksnews.com/2011/04/18/25-bizarre-scholarships).

Bellenir, Karen. College *Financing Information for Teens: Tips for a Successful Financial Life: Including Facts About Planning, Saving, and Paying for Post-Secondary Education, with Information About College Savings Plans, Scholarships, Grants, Loans, Military Service, and More*. Detroit, MI: Omnigraphics, 2008.

Carnevale, Anthony, Ban Cheah, and Jeff Strohl. "Center on Education in the Workforce." Georgetown Center on Education in the Workforce, January 4, 2012. Retrieved May 2012 (http://cew.georgetown.edu/unemployment).

Cass, Connie. "Poll: College Students Get Hard Lessons in Finance." *USA Today*, April 21, 2011. Retrieved May 2012 (http://www.usatoday.com/money/perfi/college/2011-04-23-college-students-money-poll.htm).

Chitty, Haley. Telephone interview, November 21, 2011.

Clark, Kim, and Beth Braverman. "25 Secrets to Paying For College." *Money*, April 2012, pp. 82–97.

The College Board. "Trends in College Pricing 2011." October 25, 2011. Retrieved May 2012 (http://trends.collegeboard.org/college_pricing).

Institute for College Access and Success. "Student Debt and the Class of 2010." Project on Student Debt, November 3, 2011. Retrieved May 2012(http://projectonstudentdebt.org/pub_view.php?idx=791).

Italie, Leanne. "College Application Timeline for High Schoolers." ABC News, July 12, 2011 (http://abcnews .go.com/Health/wireStory?id=14053669).

Missouri Department of Higher Education. *The Source.* Jefferson City, MO: Department of Higher Education, 2011.

Moody, Erin. "BBQ-Peanut Butter Quesadilla Wins Hilton Head Student $35,000 in Jif Recipe Contest." IslandPacket.com, March 23, 2012. Retrieved May 2012 (http://www.island-packet.com/2012/03/22/2010307/bbq-peanut-butter-quesadilla-wins.html).

National Collegiate Athletic Association. "Behind the Blue Disk." April 18, 2012. Retrieved May 2012 (http://www.ncaa.org/wps/wcm/connect/public/NCAA/Resources/Behind the Blue Disk/How Do Athletic Scholarships Work).

O'Shaughnessy, Lynn. *The College Solution: A Guide for Everyone Looking for the Right School at the Right Price.* Upper Saddle River, NJ: FT Press, 2008.

Patterson, Ashleigh. "FAFSA: Submit Early to Max Out Your Financial Aid." *Reuters,* January 14, 2011. Retrieved May 2012 (http://blogs.reuters.com/reuters-money/2011/01/14/fafsa-submit-early-to-max-out-your-financial-aid).

Pierce, Valerie, and Cheryl Rilly. *Countdown to College: 21 'To-Do' Lists for High School.* Lansing, MI: Front Porch, 2009.

Reynolds, Dean. "The Crushing Impact of Student Debt." CBS News, October 26, 2011. Retrieved May 2012 (http://www.cbsnews.com/8301-18563_162-20126148/the-crushing-impact-of-student-debt).

Scholarships.com. "Free College Scholarship Search." November 27, 2011. Retrieved May 2012 (http://www.scholarships.com).

Index

About the Author

Lisa Wade McCormick is an award-winning writer and investigative reporter. She has also written sixteen nonfiction books for children. McCormick and her family live in Kansas City, Missouri. She often visits schools and libraries with her Golden Retriever, who is a Reading Education Assistance Dog.

Photo Credits

Cover (right) © iStockphoto.com/Neustockimages; cover, pp. 1 (top left), 8, 19, 30, 42 © iStockphoto.com/Courtney Keating; cover, p. 1 (center left) © iStockphoto.com/John Cowie; cover, p. 1 (bottom left) © iStockphoto.com/Andrew Rich; cover, p. 1 (background) © iStockphoto.com/Dean Turner; pp. 4–5 iStockphoto/Thinkstock; pp. 9, 10, 34, 47 © AP Images; p. 17 © Colin Young-Wolff/PhotoEdit; pp. 20, 43 Digital Vision/ Thinkstock; p. 25 Sean Justice/Stone/Getty Images; p. 27 © Rudi Von Briel/PhotoEdit; p. 31 Boston Globe/Getty Images; p. 35 © David Young-Wolff/PhotoEdit; p. 37 Edvisors Network, Inc.; p. 39 Barry Austin Photography/Riser/Getty Images; p. 45 Marilyn Angel Wynn/Nativestock/Getty Images; p. 51 Yellow Dog Productions/Lifesize/Getty Images; p. 53 © iStockphoto. com/Vasiliy Kosyrev; interior page graphic (arrows) © iStockphoto .com/ Che McPherson; interior background image (money) © iStockphoto.com/Yekaterina Rashap.

Designer: Sam Zavieh; Editor: Bethany Bryan;
Photo Researcher: Marty Levick